PRESENTED TO:

Duncan and Fiona

BY:

Rev Thomas Nelson
Netherlee Parish Church

DATE:

23rd July 2005

THE BOOK OF
BLESSINGS
FOR COUPLES

Honor Books

07 06 05 04 03   10 9 8 7 6 5 4 3 2 1

The Book of Blessings for Couples
ISBN 1-56292-419-2

Copyright ©2003 by **Bordon Books**
6532 E. 71 Street, Suite 105
tulsa, OK 74133

Published by Honor Books,
An Imprint of Cook Communications Ministries
4050 Lee Vance View
Colorado Springs, CO 80918

Developed by Borbon Books

Manuscript written and compiled by Betsy Williams, Tulsa, Oklahoma.

INTRODUCTION

You are blessed! And as a couple, you are doubly blessed! Let's remember the precious blessings we have in our partners—their smile, the warmth of their embrace, the sound of their voice. And then, there are all the special memories you two share—times of blessing that have shaped your relationship and made you who you are as a couple.

Remember that first kiss you shared? Remember the moment when you first realized you were really in love? These blessings are God's gifts to the two of you. They are His way of saying, "I care about you. You are important to Me."

Take a moment now and enjoy this collection of quotations, prayers, poems, and meditations on the blessings of your lives as a couple. Turn the pages and remember the ways in which God's blessings have already made your lives abundant and good. And for those special occasions, prayers of blessing are included that you can say over your new home, your first child, and your golden anniversary, to name only a few.

While you are reflecting on all of these wonderful things in your lives, don't forget to remind yourselves that you are loved very much by Someone who loves to shower you with blessings.

TIME OF ROSES

It was not in the Winter
Our loving lot was cast;
It was the time of roses—
We pluck'd them as we pass'd!

'Twas twilight, and I bade you go,
But still you held me fast;
It was the time of roses—
We pluck'd them as we pass'd!

What greater blessing can we find than the
discovery that someone loves us—someone
whose opinion matters to us very much!
And greater still the blessing when we have
discovered a growing, passionate appreciation for this someone as well.

Then life is bliss.

Love puts the fun in together,
The sad in apart,
The hope in tomorrow,
The joy in the heart.

**Love doesn't make the world go round,
Love is what makes the ride worthwhile.**

Remember falling in love? What a blessing
that time of love is! Someone thinks you
are wonderful—and you? You tremble
deep inside at the thought that at last you
have found a match for you—someone
who understands you and loves you!

WAITING FOR DAISY

The girls gradually came out onto the lawn. I began to fear that Daisy was not coming. She was the last of all. I was horribly afraid she had been advised not to appear because I was there. Presently, I turned and there she was in a black velvet jacket and light dress, with a white feather in her hat and her bright golden hair tied up with blue ribbon. How bright and fresh and happy and pretty she looked. . . .

I love her more and more each time I see her. I think she loves me a little. I hope so. God grant it. . . . I fancy I can see it in her clear, loving, deep gray eyes, so true and fearless and honest—those beautiful Welsh eyes that seem to like to meet mine. I think she likes to be with me and talk with me, or why did she come back to me again and again and stand by me and talk to no one else? I wish I could tell her how dearly I love her but I dare not.

LOVE

Love is a Ride of Thrills

Did he look my way? Did she?
Will he take my hand? Will she?
Should I kiss his cheek? Should I?
Will he kiss my lips? Could I?
Will he ever ask? Dare I?

Love is a Game of Nerves

Does she love me? Does he?
Will she stay? Will he?
Can she understand? Can he?
Will she ever forgive? Will he?
Can she ever forget? Did he?

Love is a Treasure Found

Does she love me? Yes!
Will he stay? Of course!
Dare I say the words?
Oh, yes! Oh, yes! A thousand times yes!

THE STORY OF LOVE

Everyone's love is unique. You can tell this by how couples recount the first meeting, the first date, the first kiss, the first glimmer of the thought that maybe this was forever love. Every couple has their own story and it is unique. So do you. How did you meet your sweetheart? Where was that first date? When was that first kiss? When did you experience the dawning realization that yes, YES! this is the one I want to spend my life with! All these events constitute the story of your love and also the story of God's blessing on your life.

Sometimes, during hard times, it is good to remember those stories. They are the foundation of your love, and sometimes they can remind you why you thought this person, this "us" was a blessing. Love will always have to go through hard times. But love also can make it through to the other side of those hard times with yet another story of love's blessing—and love's endurance.

THE BLESSING OF ROMANTIC LOVE

What then is Love? say on.
"Two souls and one thought only,
Two hearts that throb as one."

Somewhere there waits in this world of ours
For one lone soul another lonely soul,
Each choosing each through all the weary hours,
And meeting strangely at one sudden goal.
Then blend they, like green leaves
with golden flowers,
Into one beautiful and perfect whole;
And life's long night is ended, and the way
Lies open onward to eternal day.

DATING

It's been six months, Debbie mused as she put on her mascara. *I can't believe it's going so well. I wonder if we can really go the distance?* Of all the men she had dated, Brian was by far the most mature, the one with whom she felt the most at ease. She had made her share of mistakes and consequently found it hard to believe that she could have a healthy and wholesome relationship with a man.

From the beginning, Brian was intent on developing a strong foundation of friendship with Debbie—a move that gave her peace from the start. Both had experienced past relationships that had gone sour, and both had decided that future relationships would be different. And indeed this relationship *was* different. Concentrating on getting to know one another—the good, the bad, and the ugly—they were careful not to get too swept away by emotions. Yes, they were crazy about each other, but they knew a lasting relationship had to be built on more than good feelings.

They didn't dodge difficult issues. They were honest with each other. It was working. *Who knows?* Debbie pondered. *If this is really right for both of us, this time next year I could have a ring on my finger. Oh, Father, thank You for bringing Brian into my life!*

*What a lovely filly you are, my love! How lovely your
cheeks are, with your hair falling down upon them!
How stately your neck with that long string of jewels.
We shall make you gold earrings and silver beads. . . .*

*My beloved is a bouquet of flowers in the gardens
of Engedi. How beautiful you are, my love, how
beautiful! Your eyes are soft as doves'. What a
lovely, pleasant thing you are, lying here upon the
grass, shaded by the cedar trees and firs.*

SONG OF SOLOMON 1:9–11,14–17 TLB

The beauty seen is partly in him who sees it.

Have you really looked at your partner
lately? The next time you are together,
reflect on the features you've always liked
best in them. And don't forget to tell your
sweetheart just how much you love them.

A PASSAGE OF LOVE FROM THE BIBLE

King Solomon to His Beloved

*Rise up, my love, my fair one, and come away. For
the winter is past, the rain is over and gone. The
flowers are springing up and the time of the singing
of birds has come. Yes, spring is here. The leaves
are coming out, and the grapevines are in blossom.
How delicious they smell! Arise, my love, my fair
one, and come away.*

SONG OF SOLOMON 2:10–13 TLB

*O my beloved, you are as beautiful as the lovely
land of Tirzah, yes, beautiful as Jerusalem, and how
you capture my heart. Look the other way, for your
eyes have overcome me!*

SONG OF SOLOMON 6:4–5 TLB

Love is a blazing, crackling, green-wood flame,
as much smoke as flame; friendship, married
friendship particularly, is a steady, intense,
comfortable fire. Love, in courtship, is friendship
in hope; in matrimony, friendship upon proof.

Romantic love reaches out in little ways,
showing attention and admiration. Romantic
love remembers what pleases a woman,
what excites her, and what surprises her.
Its actions whisper, "You are the most
special person in my life."

The most precious possession that ever comes
to a man in this world is a woman's heart.

HE BLESSING OF COURTSHIP

Courtship consists of a number of quiet
attentions, not so pointed as to alarm,
nor so vague as not to be understood.

**Love cannot endure indifference. It needs to be
wanted. Like a lamp, it needs to be fed out of the
oil of another's heart, or its flame burns low.**

Whether a couple is engaged or has been married for a
number of years, courtship is an essential ingredient of
a solid and satisfying love relationship. A romance that
is as fulfilling on the twenty-fifth wedding anniversary
as it was during the engagement period is an attainable
and enviable state—and it is possible, with loving effort.
Spend some time with your beloved reflecting on the
special days of your courtship, and set out to make it a
lifestyle. Why not dress up and go out for a candlelight
dinner next weekend? Or take a stroll through the
park holding hands. The same spark you once shared
can be rekindled into a vibrant flame if you will but
do the same things you did when you fell in love.
Go ahead, give it a shot. You'll be glad you did!

She is mine to have and to hold!
She has chosen between love and gold!
All the joys life can give
Shall be hers while I live,
For she's mine to have and to hold.

**Where true love burns,
Desire is love's pure flame.**

*For this reason a man will leave his
father and mother and be united to his wife,
and they will become one flesh.*

GENESIS 2:24 NIV

A BLESSING TO CELEBRATE YOUR ENGAGEMENT

May you rejoice over your engagement! May this time be full of celebration and romance, and may your heart sing the praises of the One who has brought you together. May you realize that it is ultimately God blessing you through one another, and it thrills His heart to witness your love.

May you build a firm foundation of honesty, respect, and trust as your hearts are knit together. May there be complete emotional safety as you share your hearts, and may these healthy patterns of relating serve you for the rest of your lives. May you have the inner strength to wait till your wedding night to share your gift of intimate love, and may you realize it will be well worth the wait.

Finally, may God go before you, so the wedding plans will come together smoothly. May decisions come easily, and may you have the wedding of your dreams at a budget you can live with. May you be filled with God's peace instead of stress, and may you enjoy each day of this very special time.

Amen.

THE PASSIONATE SHEPHERD TO HIS LOVE

I love thee—I love thee!
'Tis all that I can say;
It is my vision in the night,
My dreaming in the day;
The very echo of my heart,
The blessing when I pray:
I love thee—I love thee!
Is all that I can say.
I love thee—I love thee!
Is ever on my tongue;
In all my proudest poesy
Whatever be thy chance

That chorus still is sung;
It is the verdict of my eyes,
Amidst the gay and young:
I love thee—I love thee!
A thousand maids among.
I love thee—I love thee!
Thy bright and hazel glance,
The mellow lute upon those lips,
Whose tender tones entrance;
But most, dear heart of hearts, thy proofs
That still these words enhance.
I love thee—I love thee!

There are three things that are too hard for me,
really four I don't understand:
the way an eagle flies in the sky,
the way a snake slides over a rock,
the way a ship sails on the sea,
and the way a man and a woman fall in love.

PROVERBS 30:18–19 NCV

Do you remember what it felt like during the
initial stages of your relationship? How it
felt to be the pursuer? Or the one pursued?
God gave you those electrifying emotions, and
they are a blessing when shared between
two whom God has brought together. Maybe
it's been awhile since your switch has been
turned on. How about a game of hot pursuit?

A PASSAGE OF LOVE FROM THE BIBLE

Jacob and Rachel

After Jacob had been [at his uncle's house] about a month, Laban said to him one day, "Just because we are relatives is no reason for you to work for me without pay. How much do you want?" Now Laban had two daughters, Leah, the older, and her younger sister, Rachel. Leah had lovely eyes, but Rachel was shapely, and in every way a beauty. Well, Jacob was in love with Rachel. So he told her father, "I'll work for you seven years if you'll give me Rachel as my wife."

"Agreed!" Laban replied. "I'd rather give her to you than to someone outside the family."

So Jacob spent the next seven years working to pay for Rachel. But they seemed to him but a few days, he was so much in love. Finally the time came for him to marry her.

GENESIS 29:14–21 TLB

When two persons have so good an opinion
of each other as to come together for life, they
will not differ in matters of importance, because
they think of each other with respect; and in
regard to all things of consideration that may
affect them, they are prepared for mutual
assistance and relief in such occurrences.

A journal in time is a best friend to whom
everything is told and confessed. However, for
an engaged or married man to have a secret
best friend who knows things which are
concealed from his lady seems to me to be
deliberate infidelity. I am, as it were, engaged to
two women, [my journal and my wife,] and
one of them is being deceived . . . I would have
my wife know all about me, and if I cannot be
loved for what I surely am, I do not want to be
loved for what I am not. If I continue to write,
therefore, she shall read what I have written.

The wisdom that comes from heaven is first of all
pure; then peace-loving, considerate, submissive,
full of mercy and good fruit, impartial and sincere.
JAMES 3:15 NIV

THE ENGAGEMENT

Brian and Debbie were quiet, enjoying one another's company on her porch swing. Finally, Brian stopped the swing.

"I don't know what I've been waiting for," he began. "I've known almost from the beginning that you are the one I want to spend the rest of my life with, but after what we've both been through in other relationships, I knew I owed it to you—and to myself—to make sure this was right."

Debbie's face lit up. It was a moment she thought she might never have again, having once been in a disastrous relationship. But this time was different. It wasn't like a leap into the great unknown as it had been in her previous engagement, but rather this was simple—more like taking the next step on a long journey. And it indeed was a journey—*their* journey. Of course Debbie said yes. They were so right for one another and had built a solid foundation over many months. They had tackled all the big questions and knew they were compatible. They had shared their innermost dreams and fears and found safety in one another. God gave these best friends to each other, and now it was time to become one.

MY BELOVED IS MINE, AND I AM HIS

Nor time, nor place, nor chance,
nor death can bow
My least desires unto the least remove;
He's firmly mine by oath, I his by vow;
He's mine by faith, and I am his by love;
He's mine by water, I am his by wine;
Thus I my best beloved's am; thus he is mine.

He is my altar; I, his holy place;
I am his guest, and he my living food;
I'm his by penitence, he mine by grace;
I'm his by purchase, he is mine by blood!
He's my supporting elm, and I his vine;
Thus I my best beloved's am; thus he is mine.

 LOVE LETTERS

I can never be the same again. I am a different person now, praise the Lord, and you have made all the difference. My heart is in your keeping forever and ever. I live from now on to serve Him and to make you happy.

A letter from Peter Marshall to Catherine soon-to-be-Marshall.

Valentine Verse

Forget me not;
Forget me never
Until the sun
Has set forever.

It Is Love

It is love that asks, that seeks,
that knocks, that finds,
And that is faithful to what it finds.

Chains do not hold a marriage together.
It is threads—hundreds of tiny threads—
that sew people together through the years.

**There is no more lovely, friendly, or
charming relationship, communion, or
company, than a good marriage.**

All that can be called happy in the life of man
is summed up in the state of marriage;
that is the center
to which all lesser delights of life tend,
as a point in the circle.

*Marriage should be honored by all,
and the marriage bed kept pure.*
HEBREWS 13:4 NIV

A BLESSING FOR YOUR WEDDING

May this be the beginning of the most fabulous journey the two of you can imagine. May all who have witnessed your exchange of vows support you in their thoughts, prayers, words, and actions. May the memories you are making today be treasured in your hearts, and may you reflect on them often, especially during times of adversity.

May you always be kind to one another and never take each other for granted. May you be sensitive to one another's needs and find delight in serving each other. When you disagree, may you not be disagreeable. May you resolve all conflicts and never let the sun go down on your anger. May you never forget that you are on the same team and never see the other as the adversary. May you be quick to forgive and never give place to bitterness.

May your love for one another grow deeper every day, and may your union be a blessing to all who know you. May God grant you His blessing and give you peace.

Amen.

Kindness is like a rose, which though
easily crushed and fragile, yet speaks
a language of silent power.

**A man who could make one rose . . .
would be accounted most wonderful;
yet God scatters countless such flowers
around us! His gifts are so infinite
that we do not see them.**

Do you remember the occasion of the first
bouquet given by one of you to the other?
No doubt, it is a special memory, and even
now your heart likely swells as you reflect
on the romantic feelings the gesture invoked.
Few things speak of romance like the giving of
a rose. Why not give one today and include a
note celebrating the romantic love you share.

THE WHITE ROSE

The red rose whispers of passion,
And the white rose breathes of love;
O, the red rose is a falcon,
And the white rose is a dove.

But I send you a cream-white rosebud
With a flush on its petal tips;
For the love that is purest and sweetest
Has a kiss of desire on the lips.

PASSAGES OF LOVE FROM THE BIBLE

The Girl to King Solomon

*Seal me in your heart with permanent betrothal,
for love is strong as death and jealousy is as cruel
as Sheol. It flashes fire, the very flame of Jehovah.
Many waters cannot quench the flame of love,
neither can the floods drown it. If a man tried to
buy it with everything he owned, he couldn't do it.*

SONG OF SOLOMON 8:6–7 TLB

PASSAGES OF LOVE FROM THE BIBLE

The Girl about King Solomon

My beloved one is tanned and handsome, better than ten thousand others! His head is purest gold, and he has wavy, raven hair. His eyes are like doves beside the water brooks, deep and quiet. His cheeks are like sweetly scented beds of spices. His lips are perfumed lilies, his breath like myrrh. His arms are round bars of gold set with topaz; his body is bright ivory encrusted with jewels. His legs are as pillars of marble set in sockets of finest gold, like cedars of Lebanon; none can rival him. His mouth is altogether sweet, lovable in every way. Such, O women of Jerusalem, is my beloved, my friend.

SONG OF SOLOMON 5:10–16 TLB

My beloved is mine and I am his.

SONG OF SOLOMON 2:16 TLB

AN OLD IRISH WEDDING BLESSING

May God be with you and bless you
May you see your children's children
May you be poor in misfortune,
rich in blessings
May you know nothing but happiness
From this day forward

From every human being there rises a light
that reaches straight to heaven. And when
two souls that are destined to be together
find each other, their streams of light flow
together, and a single brighter light goes
forth from their united being.

THE WEDDING

Debbie's first thoughts that morning were of Brian and how thankful she was that God had brought him into her life. It was no accident that she and Brian were so well suited for one another. Only God could have arranged such a connection. They were already one in their hearts, and on that day their union would be complete.

No doubt, this was the biggest decision she had ever made, but she couldn't even imagine life without Brian. The exchange of vows was simply the next step in the journey they had begun together over a year before.

As her father walked her into the sanctuary, Debbie's eyes met Brian's; and it was as if they had entered their own private world. Planned down to the minutest detail, each part of the cer—emony told the story of the two being made one.

It had been well worth the wait for their paths to cross, well worth taking the risk to love again, and well worth the months of getting to know one another inside out. It wasn't hard to imagine God smiling as the minister declared them husband and wife.

Two persons who have chosen each other out of
all humanity, with the design to be each other's
mutual comfort and entertainment, have, in that
action, bound themselves to be good-humored,
affable, discreet, forgiving, patient, and joyful,
with respect to each other's frailties and
perfections, to the end of their lives.

Commitment is a blessing. It makes you feel
safe and secure when someone commits their
love and life to you. It also gives you the
assurance that you are loved and worthy
of their love. In no other relationship is this
deep loyalty more important than in marriage.
Why not bless your mate today by sharing
that you are committed for life to love them.

THE BLESSING OF COMMITMENT

What greater thing is there
for two human souls
than to feel that they are joined for life—
to strengthen each other . . .
to rest on each other . . .
to minister to each other . . .
to be one with each other in silent,
unspeakable memories. . . .

Moravian Covenant for Christian Living:
We regard Christian marriage as an
indissoluble union, which requires
the lifelong loyalty of the man and
the woman toward each other.

I am my beloved's and my beloved is mine.
SONG OF SOLOMON 6:3 TLB

The king lies on his bed, enchanted by the
fragrance of my perfume. My beloved one is
a sachet of myrrh lying between my breasts.

SONG OF SOLOMON 1:12–13 TLB

My lover is an apple tree, the finest in the orchard
as compared with any of the other youths. I am
seated in his much-desired shade and his fruit is
lovely to eat. He brings me to the banquet hall,
and everyone can see how much he loves me.
Oh, feed me with your love—your 'raisins'
and your 'apples'—for I am utterly lovesick.
His left hand is under my head and
with his right hand he embraces me.

SONG OF SOLOMON 2:3–6 TLB

PASSAGES OF LOVE FROM THE BIBLE

The Bride to King Solomon

*Come, north wind, awaken; come, south wind,
blow upon my garden and waft its lovely
perfume to my beloved. Let him come into
his garden and eat its choicest fruits.*

SONG OF SOLOMON 4:16 TLB

*I am my beloved's and I am the one he desires.
Come, my beloved, let us go out into the fields
and stay in the villages. Let us get up early and
go out to the vineyards and see whether the vines
have budded and whether the blossoms have opened
and whether the pomegranates are in flower.
And there I will give you my love. There the
mandrakes give forth their fragrance, and the rarest
fruits are at our doors, the new as well as old,
for I have stored them up for my beloved.*

SONG OF SOLOMON 7:10-13 TLB

Walls for the wind,
And a roof for the rain,
And drinks beside the fire—
Laughter to cheer you
And those you love near you,
And all that your heart may desire!
Bless you and yours
As well as the cottage you live in.
May the roof overhead be well-thatched
And those inside be well-matched.

By wisdom a house is built,
and through understanding it is established;
through knowledge its rooms are filled
with rare and beautiful treasures.
PROVERBS 24:3-4 NIV

A BLESSING FOR YOUR NEW HOME

May this new home be more than just a physical house, but rather may it be a home filled with life and love. May it be filled with laughter and good cheer, and may it be a place where good memories are made.

May there be harmony between us and our children to come, and may strife be turned out-of-doors. May each member of the family honor one another and may all be treated with respect. May only kind words be spoken here and harsh words never uttered. May it be a place of growth and grace, a happy dwelling place.

May light fill every chamber, and may those who live here be a beacon of hope to draw those who are weary and burdened. May every person who crosses the threshold be met with Your peace and find a safe harbor, a place of refuge. May they leave better than when they arrived, refreshed and restored.

Amen.

The first duty of a wise advocate is to convince
his opponents that he understands their arguments,
and sympathizes with their just feelings.

**I, as free, forgive you
As I would be forgiven: I forgive all.**

We all like to forgive and love best not those who
offend us least, nor who have done most for us, but
those who make it most easy for us to forgive them.

It is hard to stop a quarrel once it starts, so don't let it begin.
PROVERBS 17:14 TLB

*"In your anger do not sin": Do not let the sun
go down while you are still angry.*
EPHESIANS 4:26–27 NIV

Who's usually the first to apologize in your relationship? Being on opposite sides of the fence never solved
anything. Next time there's a conflict, why not climb
over that fence and be the first to make things right?
It will be a blessing you won't regret.

THE FIRST SPAT

This can't be happening, Debbie thought as she wiped the tears from her eyes. Three weeks into their marriage and already a disagreement. The worst part was that Brian had *left!* She knew in her head he'd probably be back, but then again she wasn't too sure. Her father had left her mother when Debbie was young, and Debbie herself had been rejected by men before. Could Brian be calling it quits?

Debbie began to pray. "Dear God, I don't understand what is happening. Please help us." Before the hour was up, Brian returned. After cooling down, he had realized the implications of his actions and rushed home to make things right. He began the dialogue.

"Honey, I didn't handle this well. I never should have walked out the door. I just needed to clear my head and calm down. But then I realized what you must have been thinking. We're on the same team, you and I, and no matter what happens, we can work it out. We've always been able to talk about everything, and this situation is no different."

The two established some ground rules that day—never walking out without an explanation was one of them. They knew there would be more disagreements, but they were both committed to play by the rules.

Husbands and wives should constantly
guard against overcommitment.
Even worthwhile and enjoyable
activities become damaging when they
consume the last ounce of energy or
the remaining free moments in the day.

A world of care without,
A world of strife shut out,
A world of love shut in.

Busyness is an enemy to the future of your
love—leisure to be with one another,
its friend. Good memories arise from
the blessing of time together. And good
memories make strong marriages.

THE BLESSING OF RESOLVING CONFLICTS

All married couples should learn the art of
battle as they should learn the art of love.
Good battle is objective and honest—never
vicious or cruel. Good battle is healthy and
constructive, and it brings to a marriage
the principle of equal partnership.

**Marriage with peace is this world's
paradise; with strife, this life's purgatory.**

*Get rid of all bitterness, rage and anger, brawling
and slander, along with every form of malice. Be
kind and compassionate to one another, forgiving
each other, just as in Christ God forgave you.*
EPHESIANS 4:31–32 NIV

A PASSAGE OF LOVE FROM THE BIBLE

King Solomon to His Bride

"How beautiful you are, my love, how beautiful!
Your eyes are those of doves. Your hair falls
across your face like flocks of goats that frisk
across the slopes of Gilead. Your teeth are white as
sheep's wool, newly shorn and washed; perfectly
matched, without one missing. Your lips are like a
thread of scarlet—and how beautiful your mouth.
Your cheeks are matched loveliness behind your
locks. Your neck is stately as the tower of David,
jeweled with a thousand heroes' shields. Your
breasts are like twin fawns of a gazelle, feeding
among the lilies. Until the morning dawns and the
shadows flee away, I will go to the mountain of
myrrh and to the hill of frankincense. You are so
beautiful, my love, in every part of you.

"Come with me from Lebanon, my bride. We will look down from the summit of the mountain, from the top of Mount Hermon, where the lions have their dens, and panthers prowl. You have ravished my heart, my lovely one, my bride; I am overcome by one glance of your eyes, by a single bead of your necklace. How sweet is your love, my darling, my bride. How much better it is than mere wine. The perfume of your love is more fragrant than all the richest spices. Your lips, my dear, are made of honey. Yes, honey and cream are under your tongue, and the scent of your garments is like the scent of the mountains and cedars of Lebanon.

"My darling bride is like a private garden, a spring that no one else can have, a fountain of my own. You are like a lovely orchard bearing precious fruit, with the rarest of perfumes; nard and saffron, calamus and cinnamon, and perfume from every other incense tree, as well as myrrh and aloes, and every other lovely spice. You are a garden fountain, a well of living water, refreshing as the streams from the Lebanon mountains."

SONG OF SOLOMON 4:1–15 TLB

THE BLESSING OF FORGIVENESS

Forgiveness is a funny thing—
it warms the heart and cools the sting.

**Once a woman has forgiven her man,
she must not reheat his sins for breakfast.**

It's very easy to forgive others their mistakes;
it takes more guts and gumption to forgive
them for having witnessed your own.

**As we practice the work of forgiveness,
we discover more and more
that forgiveness and healing are one.**

Bear with each other and forgive whatever
grievances you may have against one another.
Forgive as the Lord forgave you.

COLOSSIANS 3:13 NIV

Love is an act of endless forgiveness
A tender look which becomes a habit.

A happy marriage
is the union of two good forgivers.

A retentive memory is a good thing,
but the ability to forget
is the true token of greatness.

When you forgive you in no way change
the past—but you sure do change the future.

One pardons to the degree that one loves.

I see not a step before me as I tread on
another year; but I've left the past in
God's keeping—the future His mercy
shall clear; and what looks dark in the
distance may brighten as I draw near.

**The holiest of all holidays are those
kept by ourselves in silence and apart;
the secret anniversaries of the heart.**

Wedding anniversaries are not the only
celebrations of the heart. Can you remember
when you first met? Your first date? What
about the day you were engaged? Or what
about the day your sweetheart showed in
some special way just how much they loved
you? Celebrate these special blessings too,
even if in the silence of your heart.

A BLESSING FOR OUR ANNIVERSARY

May God bless us as we celebrate our wedding anniversary. May we look with fondness on the past year of marriage, remembering the good times, learning from the challenges. May we continue to grow closer, and may our love grow deeper each day. As our relationship continues to evolve, may we give each other room to grow and may we support each other to become all God has created us to be. May we accept one another as we are, celebrating our strengths and being patient with our limitations.

May we be sensitive to one another's needs, and may we continually look for ways to bless each other. May our intimacy continue to grow richer and more fulfilling with each passing year, and may we continue to provide a safe haven for one another.

May God direct us in our plans for the future, and may He help us carry out those plans in ways that please Him. May this next year be even better than the previous one, and may our hearts continue to be knit together as one.

Amen.

The year is closed, the record made,
The last deed done, the last word said,
The memory alone remains
Of all its joys, its grief, its gains,
And now with purpose full and clear,
We turn to meet another year.

WAYS TO CELEBRATE OUR ANNIVERSARY

Anniversaries are special days to celebrate milestones, and no milestone is more important than one's wedding anniversary. Anniversaries are times set aside for reflection and celebration, and they can be a springboard for the year to come. Your anniversary is not just another day—it's *your* day. Celebrate big! You deserve it.

Some ideas to help you celebrate your first anniversary and those to come:

- Prepare or go out for a quiet dinner together. A restaurant with a romantic atmosphere will enhance your time together and will help you focus on one another with no distractions.
- Look through your wedding album and honeymoon photos together.
- Recount your favorite experiences with your mate over the previous year.
- Dream together about the upcoming year, five years from now, and even your golden anniversary.
- Set some goals that you as a couple would like to accomplish during the next year.
- Tell your mate what you like most about them.
- Go to bed early.

Weak things united become strong.

**Love does not consist of gazing at each other,
but in looking together in the same direction.**

Marriage resembles a pair of shears, so joined
that they cannot be separated, often moving in
opposite directions, yet always punishing
anyone who comes between them.

*Live in harmony with one another; be
sympathetic, . . . be compassionate and humble.
Do not repay evil with evil or insult with insult,
but with blessing, because to this you were
called so that you may inherit a blessing.*

1 PETER 3:8–9 NIV

THE BLESSING OF HARMONY

Two pure souls fused into one by an impassioned love . . . a mutual support and inspiration to each other amid life's struggles, must know the highest human happiness; this is marriage; and this is the only cornerstone of an enduring home.

How very good and pleasant it is when kindred live together in unity! . . . For there the LORD ordained his blessing, life forevermore.

PSALM 133:1,3 NRSV

When singers sing in harmony, the result is a full, rich melody. If one sings off-key, it is hard on the ears. Marriage is a lot like that. When a couple lives in harmony, the result is a beautiful relationship full of blessing. Bless one another by "singing" on key.

Beauty may be said to be
God's trademark in creation.

**Cheerfulness and contentment are
great beautifiers and are famous
preservers of good looks.**

Beauty is the mark that God sets upon virtue.

*Your beauty should not come from outward
adornment, such as braided hair and the wearing
of gold jewelry and fine clothes. Instead, it should
be that of your inner self, the unfading beauty
of a gentle and quiet spirit, which is of great
worth in God's sight. For this is the way the
holy women of the past who put their hope in
God used to make themselves beautiful.*

1 PETER 3:3–5 NIV

SHE WALKS IN BEAUTY

She walks in beauty, like the night
Of cloudless climes and starry skies;
And all that's best of dark and bright
Meet in her aspect and her eyes:

Love doesn't seek out beauty. Love, instead,
creates beauty by its affection. There is
no more durable beauty in a woman than
that created by the enduring love and
appreciation, which her husband gives
her each day, each year, for a lifetime.

You were cute when you were twenty,
And yes, my dear, at forty-two.
But the greatest beauty I have seen,
Holds hands with me at seventy-two.

Sexiness wears thin after a while and
beauty fades, but to be married to a
man who makes you laugh every
day, ah, now that's a real treat!

Laughter is a tranquilizer with no side effects.

It is often just as sacred to
laugh as it is to pray.

The One enthroned in heaven laughs.
PSALM 2:4 NIV

Ever enjoy a good belly laugh with a friend?
Think about how good it made you feel and
how it strengthened the bond you have with
that friend. How much more enjoyable
and beneficial to laugh with your mate!
Think about those little private jokes the
two of you share. You're probably
smiling now as you think about them.

THE BLESSING OF LAUGHTER

A sense of humor is the pole that adds balance
to our steps as we walk the tightrope of life.

**Laughter adds richness, texture, and color
to otherwise ordinary days. It is a gift,
a choice, a discipline, and an art.**

Shared laughter creates a bond of friendship.
When people laugh together, they cease to be
young and old, master and pupil, and employer
and worker. They have become a single group
of human beings, enjoying their existence.

A cheerful heart is good medicine.
PROVERBS 17:22 NIV

Only in a marriage—a marriage where love
is—can sex develop into the delightfully
positive force God meant it to be. Here is
where the excitement of sex really is.
When a man and a woman make a lifelong
commitment to love and cherish each other,
they are giving themselves the time they will
need to dismantle the barriers of restraint,
shyness, defensiveness, and selfishness that
exist between all human beings. It cannot be
done in a night or with a rush of passion.
It takes time to know and be known.

Intimate love is God's idea, and He
loves it when we enjoy this blessing
with that special mate He has given us.
He wants us to delight in one another, and
there is no better "glue" to help us stick
together through the trials of life.

A PASSAGE OF LOVE FROM THE BIBLE

King Solomon to His Wife

*As Mount Carmel crowns the mountains,
so your hair is your crown. The king is
held captive in your queenly tresses.*

*Oh, how delightful you are; how pleasant,
O love, for utter delight! You are tall and slim
like a palm tree, and your breasts are like its
clusters of dates. I said, I will climb up into
the palm tree and take hold of its branches. Now
may your breasts be like grape clusters, the scent
of your breath like apples, and your kisses as
exciting as the best of wine, smooth and sweet,
causing the lips of those who are asleep to speak.*

SONG OF SOLOMON 7:5–9 TLB

Making the decision to have a child is
momentous—it is to decide forever
to have your heart go walking
around outside your body.

Not in utter nakedness,
But trailing clouds of glory do we come
From God, who is our home.

The birth of every new baby is God's
vote of confidence in the future of man.

From birth I have relied on you;
you brought me forth from my mother's womb.
I will ever praise you.

PSALM 71:6 NIV

A BLESSING FOR PREGNANCY AND BIRTH

May you rejoice together at the new life growing within you. May peace surround you as you look ahead to the future, anticipating what lies ahead. May fear be far from you, and may you be assured that your Heavenly Father will walk with you step-by-step as you approach the big day.

May you and your little one be healthy and strong, and may your baby be knit together by God himself. May your doctors and nurses be wise in their oversight, and may you receive excellent medical care. May you crave healthy foods, ones that will enhance your pregnancy, and may you gain minimal weight and be fit and trim. May you get enough rest, so your little one can grow and your strength will be renewed.

May the delivery and birth of your child go smoothly, and may pain be kept to a minimum. May you look to your Heavenly Father to see you through, assured He will never let you down. And most of all, may you be happy and full of celebration for this wonderful chapter in your lives.

Amen.

A rose can say I love you,
Orchids can enthrall,
But a weed bouquet in a chubby fist,
Oh my, that says it all!

**[A baby is] a sweet new
blossom of humanity,
fresh fallen from God's own
home to flower on earth.**

Every child born into the world
is a new thought of God, an
ever-fresh and radiant possibility.

*Children are a gift from the Lord;
babies are a reward.*
PSALM 127:3 NCV

A BUNDLE OF BLESSING

It was 3:00 A.M. Debbie was rocking little Daniel during his middle-of-the-night feeding and was reflecting on all the blessings of the last year. After two years of marriage, she and Brian had decided to start their family. What a joy her pregnancy had been. Night after night, Brian would put his face near Debbie's growing abdomen and speak to their little one forming in the womb. When they would lie in bed at night, they would place their hands on Debbie's belly to feel little Daniel kicking and squirming inside. They would imagine what he would look like, whose nose he'd have, whose eyes.

The thrill of hearing "It's a boy!" would be a treasured memory for the rest of their lives, as would all of the "firsts" she and Brian would experience through Daniel. Possibly Debbie's fondest memories were being created at that moment as she and Daniel were seemingly the only ones in the world awake at such an hour. The quiet sucking, the softness of his skin, the fresh scent of baby powder. No, it didn't get much better than this, and Debbie knew it.

What sunshine is to flowers,
smiles are to humanity.

**No life is so strong and complete,
But it yearns for the smile of a friend.**

A kind heart is a fountain of gladness, making
everything in its vicinity freshen into smiles.

**Wrinkles should merely indicate
where smiles have been.**

*O my soul, why be so gloomy and discouraged?
Trust in God! I shall again praise him
for his wondrous help; he will make
me smile again, for he is my God!*

PSALM 43:5 TLB

THE BLESSING OF A SMILE

Smile at each other, smile at your wife,
smile at your husband, smile at your children,
smile at each other—it doesn't matter who it is—
and that will help you to grow up in greater love
for each other.

**Your voice makes me tremble inside
And your smile is an invitation
For my imagination to go wild.**

Plant a word of love heart-deep in a
person's life. Nurture it with a smile and
a prayer, and watch what happens.

Husbands who have the courage to be tender
enjoy marriages that mellow through the years.

We don't naturally grow together and love
each other more. We tend to grow apart,
to grow distant. So we have to work
hard at marriage. It's the most fun
work in the world, but still it's work.

A prayer of blessing from the Bible:

*May your fountain be blessed,
and may you rejoice in the wife of your youth.
A loving doe, a graceful deer—
may her breasts satisfy you always,
may you ever be captivated by her love.*

PROVERBS 5:18–19 NIV

A DEDICATION TO MY WIFE

To whom I owe the leaping delight
That quickens my senses in our wakingtime
And the rhythm that governs the
repose of our sleepingtime,
The breathing in unison

Of lovers whose bodies smell of each other
Who think the same thoughts
without need of speech
And babble the same speech
without need of meaning.

No peevish winter wind shall chill
No sullen tropic sun shall wither
The roses in the rose garden
which is ours and ours only

But this dedication is for others to read:
These are private words
addressed to you in public.

A man of quality is never threatened
by a woman of equality.

**I would like to have engraved inside every
wedding band these words: *Be kind to
one another.* This is the Golden Rule
of marriage and the secret of making
love last through the years.**

Let us love one another, for love comes from God.
1 JOHN 4:7 NIV

Think back to the first time you realized that your
beloved accepted you just the way you were.
Remember that sense of belonging, how safe it
made you feel? How much more special is that
gift of acceptance now that you know each other,
warts and all! Have you expressed your
acceptance recently? Why not do so today.

THE BLESSING OF ACCEPTANCE

Love me without fear
Trust me without questioning
Need me without demanding
Want me without restrictions
Accept me without change
Desire me without inhibitions
For a love so free . . .
Will never fly away.

Since God so loved us, we also
ought to love one another.
1 JOHN 4:11 NIV

A PASSAGE OF LOVE FROM THE BIBLE

Adam and Eve

*The Lord God said, "It isn't good for man to be
alone; I will make a companion for him, a helper
suited to his needs." So the Lord God formed from
the soil every kind of animal and bird, and brought
them to the man to see what he would call them;
and whatever he called them, that was their name.
But still there was no proper helper for the man.
Then the Lord God caused the man to fall into a
deep sleep, and took one of his ribs and closed up
the place from which he had removed it, and made
the rib into a woman, and brought her to the man.*

*"This is it!" Adam exclaimed. "She is part of my own
bone and flesh! Her name is 'woman' because she
was taken out of a man." This explains why a man
leaves his father and mother and is joined to his wife
in such a way that the two become one person.*

GENESIS 2:18–24 TLB

A WIFE IS A BLESSING

Be thou the rainbow to the storms of life!
The evening beam that smiles the clouds away,
And tints tomorrow with prophetic ray!

Thy wife is a constellation of virtues.

What is there in the vale of life
Half so delightful as a wife,
When friendship, love, and peace combine
To stamp the marriage-bond divine?

Little things are what make life sweet.
Husbands, think of all the little things your
wife does to make your life easier, especially
things that are easy to take for granted.
These are blessings that God intended you to
have, so He sent your wife to deliver them.
How about honoring your wife by letting
her know how blessed you are to have her.

A PASSAGE OF LOVE FROM THE BIBLE

The Virtuous Woman

If you can find a truly good wife, she is worth more than precious gems! Her husband can trust her, and she will richly satisfy his needs. She will not hinder him, but help him all her life. She finds wool and flax and busily spins it. She buys imported foods, brought by ship from distant ports. She gets up before dawn to prepare breakfast for her household, and plans the day's work for her servant girls. She goes out to inspect a field and buys it; with her own hands she plants a vineyard. She is energetic, a hard worker, and watches for bargains. She works far into the night!

She sews for the poor and generously gives to the needy. She has no fear of winter for her household, for she has made warm clothes for all of them. She also upholsters with finest tapestry; her own clothing is beautifully made—a purple gown of pure linen. Her husband is well known, for he sits in the council chamber with the other civic leaders. She makes belted linen garments to sell to the merchants.

She is a woman of strength and dignity, and has no fear of old age. When she speaks, her words are wise, and kindness is the rule for everything she says. She watches carefully all that goes on throughout her household, and is never lazy. Her children stand and bless her; so does her husband. He praises her with these words: "There are many fine women in the world, but you are the best of them all!"

Charm can be deceptive and beauty doesn't last, but a woman who fears and reverences God shall be greatly praised. Praise her for the many fine things she does. These good deeds of hers shall bring her honor and recognition from even the leaders of the nations.

PROVERBS 31:10–31 TLB

God's rarest blessing is,
after all, a good woman.

**Your marriage is more than a sacred
covenant with another person. It is a
spiritual discipline designed to help you
know God better, trust Him more fully,
and love Him more deeply.**

A good wife is heaven's last, best gift to man—
his gem of many virtues, his casket of jewels;
her voice his sweet music, her smiles his
brightest day, her kiss the guardian of his
innocence, her arms the pale of his safety, her
industry his surest wealth, her economy his
safest steward, her lips his faithful counselors,
her bosom the softest pillow of his cares.

*Enjoy life with the woman whom you love all the
days of your fleeting life which He has given to
you under the sun; for this is your reward in life.*
ECCLESIASTES 9:9 NASB

A BLESSING FOR A WIFE FROM HER HUSBAND

May you be blessed for being such a blessing to me. May you be empowered to fulfill God's plan for your life, and may He fill you with His wisdom as you approach each role that you fill.

May you know how much I admire you and appreciate what you bring to our marriage. May I be the husband you need me to be, and may our relationship satisfy your needs for romance and intimacy.

May your role as a mother be filled with joy as you watch our children grow up. As they take their place in the world, may you witness abundant fruit from your faithful nurturing and training.

May you be blessed with friends, both old and new, and may you enrich one another in those relationships. May you experience success in your life's work, and may you have opportunities to exercise your areas of expertise. May you receive promotion as you continue to grow in your field.

May peace surround you to shield you from anxiety and stress. May you be filled with joy and receive the desires of your heart.

Amen.

The man who finds a wife finds a good thing;
she is a blessing to him from the Lord.

PROVERBS 18:22 TLB

Many have forgotten the value of characteristics and activities which identify the family as unique and different. They are called "traditions."

What an enormous magnifier is tradition! How a thing grows in the human memory and in the human imagination when love, worship, and all that lies in the human heart is there to encourage it.

Family traditions counter alienation and confusion. They help us define who we are; they provide something steady, reliable, and safe in a confusing world.

Family traditions are blessings that make each family unique and provide us with some of our fondest memories. Perhaps the traditions you now enjoy have been adopted from your and your beloved's childhoods. Likely, you have come up with a few that are unique to your present family. Whatever the case, instead of merely going through the motions, purpose to recognize and enjoy the blessing of your family's traditions and use them to bless one another.

THE BLESSING OF FAMILY TRADITIONS

Daniel was two years old, and Debbie wanted to start some family traditions for the holidays. She and Brian agreed—the emphasis in their home would be on the real "reason for the season," the birth of Jesus Christ. The house was filled with Christmas music and the smell of cookies baking, and they had decorated the tree—with their toddler's help, of course. Now it was time to make the birthday cake. Brian had made the suggestion: "Why not have a birthday party for Jesus?"

The idea was a keeper, and every Christmas Eve since, the Fosters have thrown a birthday party to celebrate Jesus' birthday. Red and green balloons, crepe paper, and candles are used in keeping with the Christmas and birthday theme.

As Daniel got older, the Fosters added another holiday tradition. Debbie contacts a local nursing home to inquire about visiting a resident who doesn't have any family with whom to celebrate Christmas. Debbie and Daniel pick out various toiletries, a calendar for the upcoming year, and a small gift that conveys the Christmas message. Then the Fosters take some time to spread a little holiday cheer to someone in need, someone who needs to know that Jesus is the reason for the season.

An archaeologist is the best husband
any woman can have: the older she gets,
the more interested he is in her.

Thou art an elm, my husband, I a vine,
Whose weakness, married
to thy stronger state,
Makes me with thy strength
to communicate.

A prayer of blessing from the Bible:

*May the Lord make your love to grow and
overflow to each other and to everyone else, just as
our love does toward you. This will result in your
hearts being made strong, sinless, and holy by God
our Father, so that you may stand before him
guiltless on that day when our Lord Jesus Christ
returns with all those who belong to him.*

1 THESSALONIANS 3:12–13 TLB

A BLESSING FOR A HUSBAND FROM HIS WIFE

I thank God for bringing you into my life. May He richly bless you and cause you to fulfill your destiny. May you grow in wisdom and understanding so that in all situations you know the right thing to do. May your mind be filled with creative ideas, making the world a better place because you are in it. May all your efforts be crowned with success, and may you receive promotion and financial reward as you diligently pursue your career.

May God give you strength to overcome adversity. May you be healthy and live a long life. May you be kept from temptation and protected from your enemies. May you be delivered from all harm.

May our relationship be all God means for it to be. May you understand servant leadership as you direct our household, and may we flow together as one. May we be sensitive to each other's needs, always putting the other first. And may we encourage one another, always building each other up.

May our companionship be rich and our love like the finest of wines, growing better with each passing year. May our marriage be a bit of heaven on earth.

Amen.

A HUSBAND IS A BLESSING

Thy husband is thy lord, thy life, thy keeper,
Thy head, thy sovereign;
one that cares for thee
And for thy maintenance; commits his body
To painful labor both by sea and land,
To watch the night in storms, the day in cold,
Whilst thou liest warm at home,
secure and safe.

In the love of a brave and faithful man there
is always a strain of maternal tenderness;
he gives out again those beams of
protecting fondness which were shed
on him as he lay on his mother's knee.

ORDS TO BLESS MY HUSBAND

If ever two were one, then surely we.
If ever man were loved by wife, then thee;
If ever wife was happy in a man,
Compare with me, ye women, if you can.
I prize thy love more than whole mines of gold
Or all the riches that the East doth hold.
My love is such that rivers cannot quench,
Nor ought but love from thee, give recompense.
Thy love is such I can no way repay,
The heavens reward thee manifold, I pray.
Then while we live, in love let's so persevere
That when we live no more, we may live ever.

Romantic love is a passionate spiritual–
emotional–sexual attachment between a man
and a woman that reflects a high regard
for the value of each other's person.

Romance in marriage comes from
remembering all the wonderful qualities of
your spouse and never ceasing to believe in
their ability to do great things, even after
years of knowing their faults and limitations.
It is a kind of wonder, a blessed miracle of
the heart from God. And one can ask for
the ability to love like that if it is lacking.

Isn't it wonderful to know that you belong to
your beloved and your beloved to you? When
the storms of life rage, think of what a blessing it
is to come home to the safe haven of your spouse.
The sense of belonging is a blessing indeed.

A PASSAGE OF LOVE FROM THE BIBLE

A Man and His Wife Belong to One Another

Each man should have his own wife, and each woman her own husband. The husband should fulfill his marital duty to his wife, and likewise the wife to her husband. The wife's body does not belong to her alone but also to her husband. In the same way, the husband's body does not belong to him alone but also to his wife. Do not deprive each other except by mutual consent and for a time, so that you may devote yourselves to prayer. Then come together again so that Satan will not tempt you because of your lack of self-control.

1 CORINTHIANS 7:2–5 NIV

Sexuality throws no light upon love,
but only through love can we
learn to understand sexuality.

**The expression "free love" is a
contradiction in terms. If it's free, it's
not love; if it's love, it's not free.**

Most of the so-called sexual
incompatibility in marriage springs
from the delusion that sex is an activity
when it is primarily a relationship;
if the relationship is faulty, the activity
cannot long be self-sustaining
or truly satisfactory.

THE BLESSING OF INTIMATE LOVE

The act of marriage is that beautiful and
intimate relationship shared uniquely by a
husband and wife in the privacy of their love—
and it is sacred. In a real sense,
God designed them for that relationship.

**God never intended that man could find
the true meaning of his sexuality in any
other relationship than that of the total
self-giving involved in marriage.**

*Although the man and his wife were both naked,
neither of them was embarrassed or ashamed.*
GENESIS 2:25 TLB

A healthy family is sacred territory.

The family was ordained by God before
He established any other institution,
even before He established the church.

We need not power or splendor,
Wide hall or lordly dome;
The good, the true, the tender,
These form the wealth of home.

*Our families will continue; generation
after generation will be preserved
by your [God's] protection.*
PSALM 102:28 TLB

THE BLESSING OF FAMILY

A happy family is but an earlier heaven.

God sets the lonely in families.
PSALM 68:6 NIV

True happiness and a fullness of joy can be
found only in the tender and intimate
relationships of the family. For however
earnestly we may seek success and
happiness outside the home through work,
leisure activities, or large bank accounts, we
will never be fully satisfied emotionally until
we develop deep and loving relationships.

Without respect, love cannot go far or rise
high; it is an angel with but one wing.

In submission we are free to value other
people. Their dreams and plans become
important to us. We have entered into
a new, wonderful, glorious freedom—
the freedom to give up our own rights
for the good of others.

A few conquer by fighting, but more
battles are won by submitting.

When someone respects you, doesn't it make
you stand a little taller, hold your head a little
higher? How much more when spouses
have mutual respect for one another! Why
not bless your mate by voicing those
things you most respect about them.

A PASSAGE OF LOVE FROM THE BIBLE

Respect One Another

Wives, fit in with your husbands' plans; for then if they refuse to listen when you talk to them about the Lord, they will be won by your respectful, pure behavior. Your godly lives will speak to them better than any words.

You husbands must be careful of your wives, being thoughtful of their needs and honoring them as the weaker sex. Remember that you and your wife are partners in receiving God's blessings, and if you don't treat her as you should, your prayers will not get ready answers.

And now this word to all of you: You should be like one big happy family, full of sympathy toward each other, loving one another with tender hearts and humble minds. Don't repay evil for evil. Don't snap back at those who say unkind things about you. Instead, pray for God's help for them, for we are to be kind to others, and God will bless us for it.

1 PETER 3:1–2, 7–9 TLB

Respect is intended to operate
on a two-way street.

Respect is not fear and awe; it . . . [is]the
ability to see a person as they are, to be
aware of their unique individuality. Respect,
thus, implies the absence of exploitation. I
want the loved person to grow and unfold
for their own sake, and in their own ways,
and not for the purpose of serving me.

*A man must love his wife as a part of himself; and
the wife must see to it that she deeply respects her
husband—obeying, praising, and honoring him.*
EPHESIANS 5:33 TLB

THE BLESSING OF MUTUAL RESPECT

The nearer you come into relationship
with a person, the more necessary
do tact and courtesy become.

Civilization varies with the family, and the
family with civilization. Its highest and
most complete realization is found where
enlightened Christianity prevails; where
woman is exalted to her true and lofty place as
equal with the man; where husband and wife
are one in honor, influence, and affection, and
where children are a common bond of care
and love. This is the idea of a perfect family.

*Give honor and respect to all
those to whom it is due.*
ROMANS 13:7 TLB

Children must be valued as our
most priceless possession.

I love little children, and it is
not a slight thing when they,
who are fresh from God, love us.

We began by imagining that we are
giving to them; we end by realizing
that they have enriched us.

Before you were conceived I wanted you
Before you were born I loved you
Before you were here an hour
I would have died for you
This is the miracle of life.

A BLESSING OF PARENTS FOR THEIR CHILD

May God bless you and keep you safe in all of your comings and goings. May His goodness and mercy be your constant companions; and may you grow up strong, healthy, and wise. May He grant you grace in every challenge you face and confidence that He will see you through.

May God bless the works of your hands and mind so that everything you do will prosper. And in that prosperity may you always remember that every blessing comes from Him. May you always choose the right way, and may your heart be kind, filled with compassion and mercy.

In the future, may you be blessed with a spouse who honors and loves you. May your children and your children's children bless you and follow your example as you walk with God. But above all, may you be the kind of person who enjoys the companionship of God all your life long. And may He delight in your company, both now and throughout eternity.

Amen.

[Jesus] took the children in his arms,
put his hands on them and blessed them.

MARK 10:16 NIV

If it were going to be easy to raise kids,
it never would have started
with something called labor.

Kids can frustrate and irritate their
parents . . . but the rewards of raising
them far outweigh the cost. Besides,
nothing worth having ever comes cheap.

Don't panic even during the storms of adolescence. Better times are ahead.

I call the years when our children are between
six and twelve the "golden years," not because
everything's perfect . . . but because the kids
are capable and independent. . . . They're
becoming fascinating human beings who
continually astound us and make us laugh.
And they build our self-esteem. They still
adore us for the most part, not yet having
reached that age of thinking everything we
do is dumb, old-fashioned, and irrelevant.

PARENTING

Parenting Isn't for Cowards by James Dobson is a great book title on the subject, and anyone who has children would agree. And then there's the slogan that was used to recruit for the military: "It's the hardest job you'll ever love." It's also an accurate description of raising children.

But for all the work and discipline that parenting Daniel required, nothing brought Brian and Debbie more joy. What a blessing it was to receive gifts of handpicked dandelions and special rocks. Daniel made their lives more fulfilling—and a lot more fun. The couple delighted in watching all of Daniel's firsts—his first steps, his first taste of ice cream, his first day of school. Then came Daniel's driver's license, his first job, and his graduation from high school. During the challenging times—like during the "tremendous" twos and the teenage years—these memories served to encourage the couple to hang in there.

Probably the most significant of all the events the couple went through together was when they prayed with Daniel to make Jesus his Lord and Savior. Of all their many blessings, knowing they would all make their journey together through this life and the next was by far the greatest blessing of all.

 A PASSAGE OF LOVE FROM THE BIBLE

The Love Chapter

Love endures long and is patient and kind; love never is envious nor boils over with jealousy, is not boastful or vainglorious, does not display itself haughtily.

It is not conceited (arrogant and inflated with pride); it is not rude (unmannerly) and does not act unbecomingly. Love (God's love in us) does not insist on its own rights or its own way, for it is not self-seeking; it is not touchy or fretful or resentful; it takes no account of the evil done to it [it pays no attention to a suffered wrong].

It does not rejoice at injustice and unrighteousness, but rejoices when right and truth prevail.

Love bears up under anything and everything that comes, is ever ready to believe the best of every person, its hopes are fadeless under all circumstances, and it endures everything [without weakening].

*Love never fails [never fades out or becomes
obsolete or comes to an end]. As for prophecy
(the gift of interpreting the divine will and purpose),
it will be fulfilled and pass away; as for tongues,
they will be destroyed and cease; as for
knowledge, it will pass away [it will lose
its value and be superseded by truth].*

1 CORINTHIANS 13:4–8 AMP

A home filled with love is one of life's most
precious blessings. Reflect on how this love
has blessed and impacted your life. In what
way can you express your love today?

SPRING

Spring is a time when love renews,
Arises from its winter bed and
Scatters flowers upon the land.

Spring is a time when love awakes,
Opens its eyes to the wonder of the day
And sings all night for joy.

Spring is a time when love's passion returns
After a long, cold winter spent
sending down deep roots of commitment.

Spring is a time of love!

What a wonder it is that spring with all its
warmth drives so many into each other's arms
who remained apart all through the winter cold!

There is something magical about the way the
green life pushes its way through the cold
ground of winter, something that makes me feel
love shoving its persistent way through the
cold ground of my heart to bloom for you.
How much I love you in the spring!

Spring is such a wonderful time of year, a season
of new beginnings. Reflect on how you and your
beloved have enjoyed the blessing of spring
together—walks through the park, watching the
baby bunnies scurrying about, being serenaded
by celebratory choruses of the songbirds.
Thank God for the blessing of spring!

Love is a fruit in season at all times and
within the reach of every hand.

Little deeds of kindness, little words
of love, make our earth an
Eden like the Heaven above.

Have you ever had a secret pal—someone for
whom you do special things without their
knowledge? Or have you ever been the recipient
of a secret pal's thoughtfulness? If you ever
participated in such an exercise, you know it
makes the recipient feel very special. What
thoughtful deed could you do for your sweetheart
to let them know how special they are to you?

THE BLESSING OF THOUGHTFULNESS

The whole worth of a kind deed
lies in the love that inspires it.

The happiness of life is made up of minute
fractions—the little soon-forgotten charities
of a kiss or smile, a kind look, a heartfelt
compliment, and the countless infinitesimals
of pleasurable and genial feeling.

Thoughtfulness for others, generosity,
modesty, and self-respect are the qualities
which make a real gentleman, or lady,
as distinguished from the veneered article
which commonly goes by that name.

Two are better than one,
because they have a good return for their work:
If one falls down,
his friend can help him up.
But pity the man who falls
and has no one to help him up!
Also, if two lie down together, they will keep warm.
But how can one keep warm alone?
Though one may be overpowered,
two can defend themselves.
A cord of three strands is not quickly broken.

ECCLESIASTES 4:9–12 NIV

Reflect on the blessing of each relationship
you have with the members of your family.
Bet you can't imagine life without a one of
them. Why not take a little time with each
of them to let them know how they bless you
just by being the special people they are.

PASSAGES OF LOVE FROM THE BIBLE

Family Relationships

*Wives, be subject to your husbands [subordinate and
adapt yourselves to them], as is right and fitting and
your proper duty in the Lord. Husbands, love your
wives [be affectionate and sympathetic with them] and
do not be harsh or bitter or resentful toward them.
Children, obey your parents in everything, for this is
pleasing to the Lord. Fathers, do not provoke or
irritate or fret your children [do not be hard on them
or harass them], lest they become discouraged and
sullen and morose and feel inferior and frustrated.
[Do not break their spirit.]*

COLOSSIANS 3:18–21 AMP

It is as old as the creation, and yet as young
and fresh as ever. It preexisted, still exists,
and always will exist. Depend upon it,
Eve learned it in Paradise . . . there is
something so transcendent in it.

**It is the passion that is in a kiss that
gives to it its sweetness; it is the
affection in a kiss that sanctifies it.**

Four sweet lips, two pure souls, and one
undying affection—these are love's
pretty ingredients for a kiss.

*Kiss me again and again, for your love is sweeter
than wine. How fragrant your cologne, and how
great your name! No wonder all the young girls
love you! Take me with you; come, let's run!*
SONG OF SOLOMON 1:2–4 TLB

THE BLESSING OF KISSES

A long, long kiss—the kiss of youth and love.

There is the kiss of welcome and of parting;
the long, lingering, loving, present one; the
stolen, or the mutual one; the kiss of love, of
joy, and of sorrow; the seal of promise and
receipt of fulfillment. Is it strange, therefore,
that a woman is invincible whose armory
consists of kisses, smiles, sighs, and tears?

Do you remember your first kiss with your
beloved? Sure you do. How could you forget
it! The thrill and rush of emotion is felt even
now as you reflect on that special moment.
Those feelings need not be a thing of the past.
Grab your sweetheart today and plant
another memorable, passionate kiss!

The years teach much which
the days never knew.

Be still, my soul; the Lord is on thy side;
Bear patiently the cross of grief or pain;
Leave to thy God to order and provide;
In every change He faithful will remain.
Be still, my soul; thy best,
thy Heavenly Friend
Through thorny ways leads to a joyful end.

See, I am doing a new thing!
Now it springs up; do you not perceive it?
I am making a way in the desert
and streams in the wasteland.
ISAIAH 43:19 NIV

A BLESSING FOR THE EMPTY-NEST YEARS

Although we will miss our children, may we view this chapter of our lives as a time of renewal, rather than a time of loss. They will always be our children, but may we release them to become adults and to fulfill their missions in life. May we not hold on too tightly, but send them on with our blessing and love.

May the two of us look forward with anticipation to getting to know one another all over again. May this season of love be the richest we have known, and may we focus on one another again as we did when we first fell in love. May we seek ways to comfort and bless one another, cherishing our fond memories and letting go of those that are painful. May we use our life's experiences as stepping-stones toward the future, and may we have opportunities to share the wisdom we have gained. May our latter days be even better than our former ones.

Amen.

To love a person is to learn the song
That is in their heart,
And to sing it to them
When they have forgotten.

**Marriage is the strictest tie
of perpetual friendship.**

What is a friend? A single
soul dwelling in two bodies.

Marriage has in it less of beauty but more of
safety than the single life. It has more care
but less danger. It is more merry and more
sad. It is fuller of sorrows and fuller of joys.
It lies under more burdens but it is supported
by all the strengths of love and charity,
and those burdens are delightful.

THE BLESSING OF FRIENDSHIP IN MARRIAGE

Love is like a friendship caught on fire.
In the beginning a flame, very pretty,
Often hot and fierce,
But still only light and flickering.
As love grows older,
Our hearts mature
And our love becomes as coals,
Deep-burning and unquenchable.

The best friend will probably get the best spouse, because a good marriage is based on the talent for friendship.

As a mother comforts her child,
so will I comfort you.
ISAIAH 66:13 NIV

The righteous will flourish like a palm tree,
they will grow like a cedar of Lebanon;
planted in the house of the LORD,
they will flourish in the courts of our God.
They will still bear fruit in old age,
they will stay fresh and green,
proclaiming, "The LORD is upright;
he is my Rock."
PSALM 92:12–15 NIV

The empty-nest years can be some of the richest
and most meaningful of married life. They provide
the opportunity for spouses to once again focus
their love and affection on one another—with fewer
distractions. It can also be a difficult time of
transition, leaving a vacant spot in parents' hearts.
What a blessing it is to have one another
to step into this new chapter of life together!

THE EMPTY NEST

The quiet was deafening. The only sound that could be heard was the tick-tick-ticking of the grandfather clock. She didn't know whether to rejoice at the newfound freedom of having an empty nest or cry because of the void left behind. Her last child had recently married. Now it was just the two of them again.

Sitting on her daughter's bed, she looked around the room at the familiar photos, stuffed animals, trophies, and furniture—a mixture of treasured items from childhood, adolescence, and college. Only now the room was eerily void of the spark its previous tenant had provided. Lost in her thoughts, the woman was jerked back into reality by the phone ringing.

"Hi, sweetheart," the voice spoke over the line. "What would you think about going on a real-live date tonight, just like we used to when we first met? I know of a great place we could park the car and enjoy the stars."

It really was going to be OK. She knew the empty nest was a normal chapter in life, and God would give her the grace to make the transition. Meanwhile, she had to get ready for a date.

FULFILLMENT

There is no happier life
But in a wife;
The comforts are so sweet
When two do meet.
'Tis plenty, peace, a calm
Like dropping balm;
Love's weather is so fair,
Like perfumed air.
Each word such pleasure brings
Like soft-touched strings;
Love's passion moves the heart
On either part;
Such harmony together,
So pleased in either.

What a deep, rich love those later years
of marriage yield! That deep appreciation
of the differences, that just as deep
forgiveness of the faults and shortcomings.
But above these ripened fruits of love
resides that deep abiding confidence that
you love me and I, of course, love you.

Hold my hand, my sweet
As we stroll down the street.
Hold my hand and say
You love me as much
As on our wedding day.

THE BLESSING OF GRANDCHILDREN

Your contributions to your children
and grandchildren could rank as your
greatest accomplishments in life.

**A mother becomes a true grandmother the
day she stops noticing the terrible things her
children do because she is so enchanted with
the wonderful things her grandchildren do.**

Grandchildren are the dots that connect the
lines from generation to generation.

Grandchildren are the crown of the aged.
PROVERBS 17:6 NRSV

*The mercy of the LORD is from everlasting to
everlasting upon them that fear him, and his
righteousness unto children's children.*
PSALM 103:17

THE BLESSING OF BEING GRANDPARENTS

"Love 'em and leave 'em"—it's the motto of most grand-parents. One of the blessings of being a grandparent is that they can dote all over the wee ones, and when they've gotten their fill, grandparents can deposit the children back into the care of Mom and Dad.

What a blessing grandchildren are at a season of life filled with saying good-bye to friends and loved ones who have departed this life. Grandchildren complete the circle of life, demonstrating that life begins anew with each generation. They put the zip into the golden years, and their boundless energy is catching—a true blessing indeed.

Brian and Debbie had encountered their share of chal-lenges through the years, but during the autumn of their lives, they had the chance to enjoy the blessing of grandchildren together. Daniel and his wife, Elizabeth, had two children—a boy and a girl. Seeing the world through the grandchildren's eyes was a joy they hadn't experienced since Daniel had been a boy. They agreed that nothing could make their day quite like squealing grandchildren leaping into their arms.

It had been a full life for Brian and Debbie, one filled with blessings. They knew the Source of these blessings, and it was their joy to pass this rich spiritual heritage to their son and now to their grandchildren.

True love is a durable fire,
In the mind ever burning,
Never sick, never old, never dead,
From itself never turning.

**God gave us memories that we
might have roses in December.**

A heart that loves is always young.

The golden wedding anniversary is an
important goal and milestone for all married
people. What a great time it is to reflect on
the anniversaries leading up to this one and
to celebrate those memories together.
And what a blessing it is to share your
golden years with the one you love!

A BLESSING FOR YOUR GOLDEN WEDDING ANNIVERSARY

May you be filled with joy as you celebrate this golden milestone. May you be surrounded by the love of family and friends, and may your lives together serve as an example for those who know you. May the wisdom you have gained over the years serve you well, and may you have opportunities to share that wisdom with younger generations.

May you be reminded of happy times together and why you fell in love so long ago. May you be thankful that during times of adversity, God was faithful to bring you through.

May you be strong in your bodies and blessed with good health. May your minds be sharp and never lose their edge. May your remaining years together be truly golden, and may you share eternity together in Heaven.

Amen.

To me, fair friend, you never can be old.
For as you were when first your eye
I ey'd, such seems your beauty still.

One of the good things that comes of a true
marriage is that there is one face on which
changes come without your seeing them; or
rather there is one face which you can still
see the same, through all the shadows
which years have gathered upon it.

The most wonderful of all things in life is the
discovery of another human being with whom
one's relationship has a growing depth, beauty,
and joy as the years increase. This inner
progressiveness of love between two
human beings is a most marvelous thing.

THE BLESSING OF GROWING OLD TOGETHER

Grow old along with me!
The best is yet to be,
The last of life, for which the first was made:
Our times are in His hand.

**Marriage is one long conversation
checkered by disputes.**

*Even to your old age and gray hairs
I am he, I am he who will sustain you.
I have made you and I will carry you;
I will sustain you and I will rescue you.*

ISAIAH 46:4 NIV

HOW DO I LOVE THEE? LET ME COUNT THE WAYS

How do I love thee? Let me count the ways.

I love thee to the depth and breadth and height

My soul can reach, when feeling out of sight

For the ends of Being and ideal Grace.

I love thee to the level of everyday's

Most quiet need, by sun and candlelight.

I love thee freely, as men strive for Right;

I love thee purely, as they turn from Praise.

I love thee with the passion put to use

In my old griefs, and with my childhood's faith.

I love thee with a love I seemed to lose

With my lost saints—I love thee with the breath,

Smiles, tears, of all my life!—and, if God chooses,

I shall but love thee better after death.

A FINAL BLESSING

The LORD bless you, and keep you;
The LORD make His face shine on you,
And be gracious to you;
The LORD lift up His countenance on
you,
And give you peace.

NUMBERS 6:24–26 NASB

Index of Blessings

Acknowledgments

Thomas Hood (7a,20–21), Elizabeth Barrett Browning (8b,101,124–125), Francis Kilvert (9), Maria Thusick (10, 44c,57bc;84b,100,101ab,115ab), E.F.J. von Munch Bellinghausen (12a),Edwin Arnold (12b), (Christian Nestell Bovee (14b,106bc), Samuel Richardson (16a), Charles Stanley (16b), Josiah Gilbert Holland (16c), Lawrence Sterne (17a), Henry Ward Beecher (17b,56a), Will A. Heelan (18a), Samuel Taylor Coleridge (18b,42a,105b), Tatler (24a), W.N.P. Barbellion (24b), Francis Quarles (26), Augustine of Hippo(27c), Daniel Defoe (27), Simone Signoret (28a), Martin Luther (28b,30b), Daniel Defoe (28c), Francis J. Roberts (30a), John Boyle O'Reilly (31), Author Unknown (34ab,45b,59a,64a,67b,88,96a,110a), Joseph Addison (36a), George Eliot (37a,82b), Moravian Covenant for Christian Living (57b), Irish Blessing (40a), William Shakespeare (42b,80b,82a,120a,122a), Samuel Butler (42c), James C. Dobson (44a,78a,92a,94a,96bc,118a), Dora Greenwell (44b), Ann Landers (45a), William Arthur Ward (48a), Marlene Dietrich (48b), Jessamyn West (48c), Agnes Sanford (48d), Peter Ustinov (49a), Robert Quillen (49b), Elbert Green Hubbard (49c,90c), Bernard Meltzer (49d), François , Duc de la Rochefoucauld (49e), Mary Gardiner Brainard (50a), Henry Wadsworth Longfellow (50b), Robert Browning (52,123a), Proverb (54a), Antoine de Saint-Exupery (54b), Sydney Smith (54c), Elizabeth Cady Stanton (55a), Charles Dickens (56b), Ralph Waldo Emerson (56c,108a), Lord Byron (57a,75a,84,107a), Joanne Woodward (58a), Arnold Glasgow (58b), Charles R. Swindoll (58c), Tim Hansel (59b), William Grant Lee (59c), Colleen Townsend Evans (60a), Elizabeth Stone (62a), William Wordsworth (62b), Imogene Fey (62c), Gerald Massey (64b), Kate Douglas Wiggin (64c), George Addison (66a), Wallace Bruce (66b), Washington Irving (66c), Mark Twain (66d), Mother Teresa (67a,102a), Max L. Lucado (67c), Brendan Francis (68a), Anne Ortlund (68b), T.S. Eliot (69), Jill Brisco (70a), Randolph Ray (70c), Dick Sutphen (71), William Congreve (75b), William Cowper (75c), George Meredith (76a), Gary Thomas (76b), Jeremy Taylor (76c,110d), Thomas Carlyle (78b), Susan Lieberman (78c), Agatha Christie (80a), Nathaniel Branden (84a), Eugen Rosenstock-Huessy (86a), David Watson (86b), Sydney J. Harris (86c), Tim LaHaye (87a), Al Martin (87b), Billy Graham (88a), Sarah J. Hale (88b), Sir John Bowring (89a), James J. Jones Ph.D. (89c), Alexandre Dumas (90a), Richard J. Foster (90b), Erich Fromm (92b), Oliver Wendell Holmes (93a), William Aikman (93b), Charles Dickens (94b), Pope John Paul II (94c), Maureen Hawkins (94d), Vicki Lansky (96d), Julia A. Fletcher Carney (102b), Talmud (103a), Thomas Henry Huxley (103c), Thomas C. Haliburton (106a,107b), Katharina von Schlegel (108b), Samuel Johnson (110b), Aristotle (110c), Bruce Lee (111a), Friedrich Nietzsche (111b), William Cavendish (114), Lois Wyse (118bc), Sir James M. Barrie (120b), Greek Proverb (120c), George Macdonald (122b), Sir Hugh Walpole (122c), Robert Louis Stevenson (123b).

Additional copies of this title are available
from your local bookstore.

If you have enjoyed this book,
or if it has impacted your life,
we would like to hear from you.

Please contact us at:

Honor Books
An Imprint of Cook Communications Ministries
4050 Lee Vance View
Colorado Springs, CO 80918

Or by e-mail at www.cookministries.com